To Amanda

How Did You Do It, Truett?

Truett?

A Recipe for Success

S. Truett Cathy

How Did You Do It, Truett?
A Recipe for Success

Copyright © 2007 STC Literary, LLC

Written in collaboration with Dick Parker
Published by Looking Glass Books, Inc.
Decatur, Georgia

Manufactured in Canada

ISBN 978-1-929619-33-7

BERKSHIRE HATHAWAY INC.
1440 KIEWIT PLAZA
OMAHA, NEBRASKA 68131
TELEPHONE (402) 346-1400

WARREN E. BUFFETT, CHAIRMAN

June 27, 2006

Mr. S. Truett Cathy
Founder and Chairman
Chick-fil-A, Inc.
5200 Buffington Road
Atlanta, GA 30349-2998

Dear Truett:

I enjoyed both your letter and the annual report. I particularly liked your comments about being 85 with a lot of good years ahead. You and I have the same philosophy toward life.

With the fun you are having with your business, you are 100% right in not selling it. How could the world be any better?

Your offer of a Chick-fil-A sandwich is powerful – particularly with the added salt thrown in. Keep a seat reserved for me at your lunch table.

Truett, I really admire what you've accomplished. And with you at the helm, the best is yet to come.

Best regards.

Sincerely,

Warren E. Buffett

WEB/db

How Did You Do It, Truett?

A Recipe for Success

Preface
A Recipe for Success

Have you ever eaten a spoonful of lard? What about a cup of sifted flour or a cup of sugar? Or maybe a couple of raw eggs? Probably not, but everybody has enjoyed a delicious cake—the result of mixing those ingredients together in the right proportion and baking them.

When I was a boy, on a rainy Sunday afternoon I would go into my mother's kitchen to bake a cake, and I learned the importance of having all the right ingredients. If I didn't have a necessary ingredient to complete the cake, I might try a substitute. Sometimes it worked, and sometimes I made a flop.

Building a business is like that. It takes all the right ingredients—everybody in all places of responsibility doing their jobs. Some people think a good concept is most important or a good product. Others think it's the location or the team or the marketing plan. They're all right. It's all these things, and more.

Often times when we experience success at Chick-fil-A, I pat myself on the back and congratulate myself for the accomplishment. Then I have to remind myself, "Truett, *you* didn't do it. God did it, along with high-quality people at Chick-fil-A who have great ideas and work extremely hard to make the business successful, and our loyal fans, who are just as important to our success.

When I began working on this book I asked those working in Chick-fil-A restaurants and at our corporate headquarters about the ingredients to our success. Some of their comments are presented in boxes labeled "How Truett Did It" and in sidebar statements.

1

SUCCESS BEGINS
WHEN YOU REALLY *Want To*

—⟶—

I read the book as fast as I could, but I was only halfway down the page when the boy beside me turned to the next page. It was the 1930s, and we shared schoolbooks because there wasn't enough money for all the students to have their own. My teacher paired me with an A student, and no matter how fast I read, he always turned the page before I was ready. Every time the page turned, my self-concept fell a notch.

Seventy-five years later, I remember my difficult school days whenever I speak to a graduating class. "How many of you are straight-A students?" I ask. A group of hands goes up, and I say, "Well, too bad for you. I understand the world is run by C students."

And that's true. When you read the history

books about outstanding individuals, you see that
many of them didn't have brilliant minds. Instead,
they had common sense and worked hard to ac-
complish their goals. I'm sure a lot of them were
like me when they were young—slow readers and
slow learners. I didn't have
much confidence in my
ability.

When I was young, I learned that the harder you work, the more successful you will be. That still holds true today.

My parents didn't have
a lot of money, so I knew
that if I wanted nice
things—and I did—the only way to get those things
was to work hard and save my money. I explain
that simple formula for success whenever somebody
asks me, "How did you do it, Truett?"

In those difficult days of the Great Depression,
financial success meant just making a living. If you
had a regular income, you were considered a
wealthy person. So when I thought about how I
might make my living as an adult, I considered the
possibilities that would allow me to earn enough
money to take care of the family I hoped to have
someday. Ultimately I decided to open a restaurant,
but it could just as easily have been a service station
or a grocery store. I liked the idea of building some-

thing and owning it. A lot of people thought like that in the 1940s. Tom Brokaw called ours "The Greatest Generation," and he said of us:

> They came of age during the Great Depression and the Second World War and went on to build modern America—men and women whose everyday lives of duty, honor, achievement, and courage gave us the world we have today.

The NBC News anchor interviewed dozens of people to write *The Greatest Generation*, and most of them told him something along the lines of, "I just did what I had to do." We didn't dream big dreams. We didn't set out to become heroes or create the greatest economic expansion the world has ever seen. We simply took care of our families and ourselves, built with quality, and tried to look out for our neighbors.

HARD WORK AND OPPORTUNITIES

Through the years I've had hundreds of people ask me how I could start from where I did and build a company with sales of nearly $3 billion. I tell them first that I didn't begin with that goal in mind. For twenty-one years before I opened the first Chick-fil-A restaurant, I operated the Dwarf House restaurant in Hapeville, Georgia, scrambling eggs and flipping hamburgers. The success of my own restaurant fulfilled my childhood expectations of generating enough income to take care of my family. I loved my customers and the people who worked with me, and if I had never built another restaurant, I think I would have been satisfied. The Dwarf House generated enough income for us to live comfortably on a 262-acre farm south of Atlanta.

Then over the course of a few years I created several opportunities that were magnified by changes in the way Americans lived. All of those things taken together led to the creation of Chick-fil-A and set us on a path that nobody could have predicted.

How Dad was able to make the kinds of transitions you need to make in his thought processes on how you work and operate to go from flipping burgers and scrambling eggs in a mom-and-pop business called the Dwarf House to being CEO of a nearly $3 billion business—that is remarkable.
     —Dan Cathy, President and Chief Operating Officer, Chick-fil-A, Inc.

How did you learn to cook?

—ɯ—

At my mother's side. Mother ran a boarding house when I was growing up, and every afternoon she cooked supper for our boarders. My sisters were all good cooks too. My jobs in the kitchen were to shuck corn, shell peas, set the table, and wash dishes. Boarders loved Mother and loved her food. She never used a recipe. She had cooked for so long, she relied on instinct when it came to ingredients. I watched her and helped her, and sometimes on Sunday afternoons she let me bake a cake by myself. Of course, I didn't have her experience in the kitchen, so I followed the recipe carefully, as long as we had all the ingredients. When we didn't, I would ask Mother, and she would explain how I could substitute something we had in the kitchen for a missing ingredient.

The first opportunity I created was the Chick-fil-A Chicken Sandwich. It was a simple concept—a boneless, skinless breast of chicken on a toasted buttered bun with two pickles—but the recipe was years in the making.

Then in 1967 I decided to open the first Chick-fil-A restaurant in Atlanta's first shopping mall, Greenbriar Shopping Center. Nobody knew then that the shopping mall concept was about to sweep across America and that Americans were changing their shopping habits to spend many hours in those malls. Neither did anybody know that the eating habits of Americans were about to undergo a tremendous change. Over three decades, beginning in 1970, consumption of beef per person dropped 15 percent, while consumption of poultry more than doubled, according to the U.S. Department

When Dad came home from work—and he worked a ten- or twelve-hour workday—he got us out there to help him put up a barbed-wire fence or hoe an acre garden. He wanted us to learn the importance of hard work, and at the same time the physical labor helped him get rid of stress.

—Bubba Cathy
Senior Vice President,
Chick-fil-A, Inc., and
President, Dwarf House, Inc.

My most satisfying day is the day I work the hardest—the day I get the most accomplished. I think most people are that way. When they do something less than what they are capable of doing, it's work. When they do an outstanding job in their performance, it's rewarding to them.

of Agriculture. These were the same years that Chick-fil-A experienced tremendous growth, from six restaurants to nine hundred fifty-eight!

Some people look at what has happened and say we were lucky. There may be some luck involved, but I'm not sure how much. If you examine "luck," you will usually find that the people who have been lucky have also worked hard, understood the value of a dollar, and taken advantage of unexpected opportunities.

Truett has an uncanny ability to see things others don't.
—Dr. Charles Q. Carter
Pastor, Retired
First Baptist Church,
Jonesboro, Georgia

I have a friend in Helen, Georgia, who laid bricks for thirty years. After he retired he sold a piece of property in Gwinnett County, Georgia, for six times as much as he had earned all those years. You might say my friend was lucky, but I think it took common sense to buy the real estate in the first place and to hold onto it through the years while the value increased. There must have been times along the way when he was tempted to sell it and use the money to take care of other financial obligations, but he worked a little harder so he could hold onto the land until the right buyer with the right opportunity came along.

As we built Chick-fil-A over the years, the unexpected opportunities we encountered created many complex situations. The company grew to what it is today because of hard working people who understood the complexities of operations, legal, marketing, personnel, real estate and other issues that challenged us. Every day, though, we remember that the Chick-fil-A Chicken Sandwich is really a simple concept. We take advantage of our biggest opportunities when we keep it simple, focusing on serving great tasting food in a clean, wholesome environment with great customer service.

> *Truett has a God-given innate business sense that you don't learn in school.*
> *—Buck McCabe*
> *Senior Vice President and Chief Financial Officer, Chick-fil-A, Inc.*

That hasn't changed in the sixty-one years that I've been in the restaurant business.

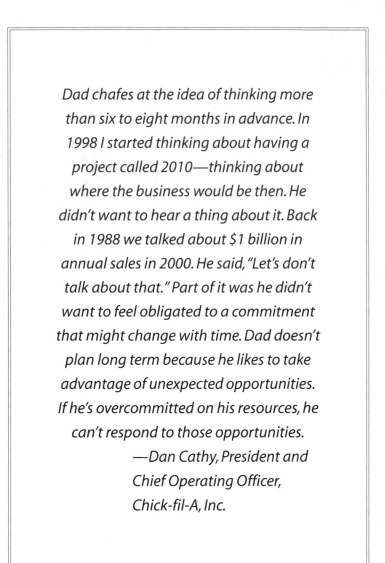

Dad chafes at the idea of thinking more than six to eight months in advance. In 1998 I started thinking about having a project called 2010—thinking about where the business would be then. He didn't want to hear a thing about it. Back in 1988 we talked about $1 billion in annual sales in 2000. He said, "Let's don't talk about that." Part of it was he didn't want to feel obligated to a commitment that might change with time. Dad doesn't plan long term because he likes to take advantage of unexpected opportunities. If he's overcommitted on his resources, he can't respond to those opportunities.

—Dan Cathy, President and Chief Operating Officer, Chick-fil-A, Inc.

2
TIMING AND SACRIFICE

—⟋⟍—

A close friend at church told me recently that he strongly felt the Lord leading him to start a new business. My friend is in his fifties and has eight children. His wife homeschools their children, so he is the sole breadwinner. When I asked him what his plans were, he said he wasn't sure. He only knew that God had been speaking to him through Scripture and through our minister's sermons, making it clear that He wanted him to start a business. He has now left his full-time job. While he seeks direction and a clearer call, his family is drawing on his retirement savings, a very costly situation.

I told my friend that I admired his faith, but I questioned his timing. There is a time and a place for everything. If you are burdened with obligations and debt—you have a family, a mortgage, and a car payment—it may be the wrong time to start thinking about establishing a business.

Truett has a tremendous ability to totally focus. He is not easily distracted. It doesn't matter what it is. He can be in the car driving, and he won't have the air conditioner on. If he's concentrating, he won't be conscious of temperature in the car. He focuses on whatever he's thinking about.
    —Jimmy Collins
    Former President,
    Chick-fil-A, Inc.

I'm not suggesting that everyone who starts a business has to follow my model, but just as in saving money, the earlier in life you start, the better your chance for success.

I was twenty-five years old and single when my youngest brother Ben and I started the Dwarf Grill (which we later renamed the Dwarf House) restaurant in Hapeville, Georgia, just south of Atlanta. World War II had just ended, and I knew if I ever was going to start a business, that was the time to do it. I didn't owe any money; I even had a little money in the bank. And because I didn't yet have a family, I could devote myself completely to the success of the business.

We all know that the scorecard of any business is the profit it produces. Without profit, we cannot take care of our employees, our families, or contribute to the betterment of our communities. The question is: How do we balance the pursuit of profit and personal character? For me, I find that balance by applying Biblical principles. I see no conflict between Biblical principles and good business practices.

Ben and I didn't have nearly enough money to build a restaurant, even at 1946 prices. I was going to have to sacrifice my time—today people call it investing "sweat equity"—and some "luxuries." The most obvious luxury I sacrificed was the new Chevrolet I had recently bought. I sold it and combined it with all the money I had saved. I now had

> **How Truett Did It**
> He did his best then trusted
> God with the rest.

$4,000 cash. Then Ben and I borrowed $6,600 from the bank. That $10,600 seemed like all the money in the world to us, but the restaurant we built with it was quite modest.

The next time you walk into a Chick-fil-A restaurant, look closely at the material and craftsmanship that went into its construction. Look behind the counter at the gleaming equipment. If you're in a stand-alone restaurant, consider the location. You're likely looking at about a $3 million investment in real estate, construction, and equipment.

To build a restaurant in 1946 comparable to today's brand-new Chick-fil-A stand-alone restaurant, Ben and I would have invested more than $250,000 (figuring for inflation)—an impossible sum of money in 1946. Even if we could have borrowed that much from the bank, we couldn't have made the payments, and we would have been bankrupt within a matter of months.

He did everything from preparing food to washing dishes to scrubbing floors. It was a small operation, and Mr. Cathy was there every day. I was impressed with the manner in which he treated people. He respected us and we respected him. And no job was too large or too small for him to do.

—Eddie White
Dwarf House employee
1940s and '50s
Retired Educator and
Administrator, Clayton
County, Georgia, Schools

To succeed we knew we had to start small and grow slowly. This is where so many start-up companies today make their mistake. Dreamers dream big, and they want to reach their goals quickly. There's nothing wrong with big dreams. But my experience tells me that we're more likely to reach our dreams if we climb with care and caution, putting one foot in front of the other.

To some, this may be the biggest sacrifice of all—giving up the dream of instant "success." But the reward for your sacrifice will be many nights of restful sleep knowing that you have positive cash flow, money in the bank, and a growing enterprise—even if it is growing slower than you would like.

Ben and I started working on the restaurant weeks before we opened, helping with construction. We dug the ditches that became the footings for the foundation. We hired a carpenter on a cost-plus-10 percent arrangement. Because the war had just ended a few months before we started construction, domestic building supply lines were not yet re-started, and I had to scramble around to find building materials. I bought a lot of used lumber for framing—sturdy wood that would be hidden behind the walls of the restaurant. We saved additional money by finding used equipment for the kitchen. We opened small—first day sales were $58.20—and grew steadily.

GIVING IT AWAY

My friend J.D. Graham worried about us in those early days. J.D. had been my route manager

When we're fully committed to something, we're not likely to give up or be discouraged. It works in our business life as well as in our personal relationships and our relationship to Jesus Christ. When you're fully committed, you see strange and unusual things happen that otherwise wouldn't if you were not committed. That's been a key to my life, a key to success. When you're fully committed, you're not likely to fail.

when I threw newspapers as a teenager, and he had helped us on the construction site. He came into the restaurant often, and he told me many times that I was giving away too much food. If I didn't start charging people, he said, we would go out of business.

J.D. was exaggerating, but I did give away a lot of food. That was the best way I knew to attract customers to a new restaurant and make friends. Everybody loves free food. Once we got customers in the door, we knew we could keep them with good service and good food. That model—offering free food to get people to try us out—would become our model for building a customer base at Chick-fil-A twenty years later.

3
IDENTIFYING THE PRODUCT

—⚊—

You've heard people say, "There are no problems, only opportunities." Well, for me, chicken was a problem that became an unexpected opportunity.

We had to take special care at the Dwarf House to make sure fried chicken was prepared properly, especially drumsticks. If you didn't cook it just right, you might still have a little blood down next to the bone. Often customers, believing that a little bit of blood indicated the chicken wasn't cooked enough, would send it back and ask for another piece. So the problem wasn't the chicken, it was the bone.

Since the first day we opened in 1946, I had cut our own steaks, and I was just as comfortable cutting up a whole chicken for frying. I decided to try cutting out the chicken bone to see how it would fry up, and it worked nicely with the breast meat.

At about the same time in the late 1950s, airlines had started serving boneless chicken breast pieces for their in-flight meals. The pieces had to be cut just the right size to fit the plastic serving trays, and sometimes the poultry companies had pieces left over that were a little too small or a little too big.

When I contacted the owners of Goode Brothers Poultry, a supplier for Delta Air Lines, Jim and Hall Goode brought some of the pieces to me at the restaurant to experiment with. The first piece I fried was ready so fast, I knew we were on to something. Not only did the boneless breast pieces cook fast, they cooked evenly. The only problem was that Goode Brothers left the skin on, and the first bite you took, the skin slid right off. So I asked them for boneless breasts with no skin, and that solved one problem and created another. A lot of the flavor of fried chicken is in the skin, so I had to develop a recipe that would give boneless, skinless breast meat more flavor.

Listening to My Customers

One of the first things I learned in the restaurant business, many years before I started working with boneless chicken breasts, was to find out what my customers wanted then provide it for them. Today we call it "consumer research." Back then I just called it "knowing my customers." So when I tried various ways of preparing the boneless, skinless chicken breasts, I always offered samples to customers and asked for their opinions.

Truett has always been interested in innovation; he's always looking for better ways to do things. He has a natural curiosity about how to do things better and differently.

—Jimmy Collins
Former President,
Chick-fil-A, Inc.

I tried a lot of different seasonings, and each time I changed the recipe, I asked customers how they liked it and what they thought I might change to make it better. After a couple of years experimenting, I was using more than twenty ingredients. (That was in the day that Colonel Sanders was touting his eleven secret herbs and spices.) I wanted the flavor to be unique and difficult for somebody to copy.

I knew I wanted a sandwich because many of

our customers were workers from all three shifts at the nearby Ford assembly plant and from Delta Air Lines headquarters. They had to eat quickly and get back to work.

Sliced bread didn't stand up to the chicken, so I tried it on a hamburger bun. And mayonnaise got hot and kind of dissolved away, so I tried butter.

As I closed in on the right recipe for the meat, customers told me they wanted just a bit more zest. Instead of adding more spice to the seasoning, I tried two dill pickles. My customers loved it. They said it was the perfect finishing touch. So the boneless breast of chicken sandwich was born.

THE RIGHT OIL

Nobody asked me in 1967 how much trans fat was in the original Chick-fil-A Chicken Sandwich. If they had, I wouldn't have been able to answer them. It was many years later that customers began to ask about the fat and calorie content of their food.

I selected peanut oil for cooking our chicken because it was the most desirable product and was low in calories. Today we know that the 100 percent refined peanut oil we have always used is not par-

*The name Chick-fil-A captures the
essence of what we do. It has forced the
organization to be very disciplined and
stay focused on chicken—the best part of
the chicken. After forty years you could
make a good argument that it was a
stroke of genius—the name and how it
has protected our focus.*

> *—Steve Robinson*
> *Senior Vice President and*
> *Chief Marketing Officer,*
> *Chick-fil-A, Inc.*

tially hydrogenated. So our chicken is trans fat free.

Something else I learned from my mother has enhanced the quality from the beginning. When she fried chicken, she used a cast-iron skillet with an iron lid that sped up the cooking process and sealed in the natural juices and flavor. I did the same thing in the Dwarf House until I learned about pressure fryers, which allowed us to cook a boneless chicken breast in four minutes.

THE RIGHT NAME

Now that I had a product, I had to come up with a name for it. For several years I called it a Chicken Steak Sandwich. In fact, the newspaper ran an special section when we opened our new Dwarf House restaurant in Forest Park in 1962. A photograph on page one shows our sign advertising DWARF BURGERS and CHICKEN STEAK SANDWICHES.

I talked to a lawyer about getting a trademark for the name "Chicken Steak Sandwich," but he said a trademark name had to be unique in some way. If I used common words, I would have to spell it in my own way.

For days I thought about the sandwich and what made it unique. It was boneless, like a boneless beef

How do you cook the chicken so quickly?

—ɯ—

I remembered my mom used a pressure cooker sometimes to make food cook faster. I experimented a bit with pressure on our deep fryer by devising a lid to fit over it and hold in the steam while it cooked. About that time the kitchen equipment manufacturers introduced controlled low-pressure fryers. The process cooked the chicken much faster and sealed in the natural juices, making it tastier. Today, using the Henny Penny fryer, we cook our boneless breasts of chicken in four minutes. The fast cooking time gives us the flexibility to hand-bread every piece of chicken, and we don't have to cook ahead of time and hold food in a warming cabinet waiting for customers.

tenderloin fillet. And like a beef fillet, our chicken was from the best part, the breast. So I let the words *chicken fillet* roll around in my head. I shortened *chicken* to *chick*, and I liked the sound of it. Chick fillet. That still wasn't quite right, though. Then one day I could see in my mind a capital *A* at the end of the word, so instead of fillet, it became "fil-A." That A stood for the best, Grade A, product. Chick-fil-A. The lawyer agreed that the name was unique, and in 1963 he got the trademark registered for me. Then I worked with a designer to create the logo, which has changed very little in more than forty years.

I realized if Chick-fil-A was going to mean anything, I had to have direct control of the product to maintain our quality.

SELLING THE SANDWICH

We sold the sandwiches in the Dwarf House restaurant, and my original business plan was to license other restaurants to sell Chick-fil-A Sandwiches, like Coca-Cola has its products sold in restaurants. I knew that plenty of restaurant owners would attend the Southeastern Restaurant Trade Association convention, so in 1964 I had a display created for the sandwich and I took some equipment to the show and cooked samples. That one event jump-started my efforts, and before long I had more than fifty restaurants and several hotels selling Chick-fil-A Sandwiches. Even Waffle House, which had about a dozen restaurants at that time, put our sandwich on their menu.

We also introduced our sandwich at the National Restaurant Association meeting in Chicago, but they didn't get very excited about us back then. I'm not sure they even understood the potential of a boneless chicken sandwich. It was a hamburger-focused world, and McDonald's was the going thing. I knew all along that even a great product wouldn't sell itself. I was going to have to work hard to get people to recognize Chick-fil-A. Many people couldn't even pronounce it. They called it *chickafill* or *chickafellow* or *chickbuffet* or *Chevrolet*.

I continued calling on restaurants to get them to sell our product. They bought their chicken from Goode Brothers and the coating and spice mixture from us. Then Goode Brothers paid us what amounted to a royalty for the chicken they sold for sandwiches.

It wasn't long, though, before I learned that

some of the restaurants selling Chick-fil-A Sandwiches didn't have the same commitment to quality that we did. I walked into a restaurant where they had cooked all the chicken first thing that morning, then left it warming all morning until the lunch crowd came in. I knew then that if I wanted our product to be known for quality, we were going to have to cook it ourselves.

> **How Truett Did It**
> Truett has focused on keeping the food menu and operations consistent and simple over the past sixty years, always focusing on the Chick-fil-A Sandwich.

A Simple Process

Our process for cooking the Chick-fil-A Chicken Sandwich hasn't changed since I developed the recipe more than forty years ago. We start with the highest quality fresh boneless chicken breast. In the restaurant the breast is opened by hand to make sure it's completely unfolded then hand-breaded before cooking. Nothing comes to us prebreaded or partially cooked.

Preparing the sandwich is a simple process—any sixteen-year-old can learn it. The real key to a perfect sandwich is high-quality, on-site leadership. Because almost all Chick-fil-A franchised Operators have only one restaurant, they're in the store virtually every day and have the best interests of their particular restaurant in mind. They care about the quality of people on their team and the quality of the food they serve. Better people and better food mean higher sales and higher profits for the Operator.

Truett Cathy's business model is profoundly simple and powerfully productive.
—Tim Tassopoulos
Senior Vice President, Operations, Chick-fil-A, Inc.

Smart Decisions Require Time

Chick-fil-A customers know we are very deliberate when it comes to introducing new products. When we introduced the Cool Wraps, in 2001, it was our first new entrée introduction since Chick-fil-A Chick-n-Strips in 1995.

Ideas for new products come from Operators, staff members, and customer surveys. For example, we introduced Chick-fil-A Nuggets in 1982 after a long testing period. One of our Operators suggested that smaller chicken pieces that people could eat with a toothpick would be popular for company holiday parties. The first suggestion was to sell the pieces in quantities of five and ten pounds.

Our team began its research by contacting people we thought would want to buy small chicken pieces: party planners. They learned that the product was desirable, but customers didn't have any idea how many pounds to order for a party. They could estimate, though, how many pieces they would need per person and buy the right amount. So we decided to sell by the piece instead of by the pound.

Before long customers were telling us they wanted Chick-fil-A Nuggets in single meal amounts in the restaurants. Through more customer trials we learned that they wanted the same amount of chicken that we served in the Chick-fil-A Chicken Sandwich. We introduced Chick-fil-A Nuggets in meal-size portions, and the product was an instant hit. After still more research, though, we found that some customers were buying two orders—one wasn't quite enough—so we introduced a larger portion size.

Then moms told us that their children loved our Chick-fil-A Nuggets, so they became the backbone of our Kids Meals.

So, just like when I developed the Chick-fil-A Chicken Sandwich by sharing samples with my customers at the Dwarf House restaurant, we introduce new products today only after letting our customers try it out in test conditions in a few restaurants throughout the chain.

Chick-fil-A Waffle Potato Fries are one more example of the process. Our marketing group felt the traditional shoestring fries we were serving were like everybody else's, and they didn't reflect the quality of Chick-fil-A. We had the best sandwich in the quick-serve category, and we wanted our fries to match that.

We went to a couple of companies we were buying shoestring potatoes from and said we needed something innovative, high quality, and different that was more nutritious than traditional fries.

One company had just perfected technology for

double-cutting the potato, and they offered samples. We took them to hundreds of customers and taste panels with two questions in mind: will we sell more of them, and will they strengthen the Chick-fil-A brand? In all of our taste panels the answer to both questions was *yes*. Then we went to restaurants and tested the product for the better part of two years, and the results were overwhelming. The decision was easy, and Chick-fil-A Waffle Potato Fries have been an important signature of our menu ever since.

4
Courtesy Pays Dividends

—ɯ—

Be kind to your customers. It's the key to success. Like the Biblical commandment to love your neighbor as yourself, all the other instructions for success in the restaurant business—or any business—hang on this one. You can't beat the Golden Rule as a business philosophy: Do unto others as you would have them do unto you.

The theme of our annual business seminar for Chick-fil-A frahcnise Operators one year was, "Courtesy is cheap, but it pays great dividends." Courtesy begins by giving you a positive mental attitude about everything you do.

Recently a customer called and said the most outstanding thing had happened to him. He was a regular at the Chick-fil-A Dwarf House restaurant in

Fayetteville, Georgia, and after he finished his meal his waiter told him, "I'm going to pay this bill for you."

The kinder you are to your people, the more productive they will be, and the more customers you'll be able to attract.

The customer was astounded. Nothing like that had ever happened to him. He asked the waiter if he had understood correctly, and the young man said, "It's my Christmas gift to you."

I was in the restaurant a short time later and saw the young waiter. I asked him why he had done such a thing, and he said, "Just out of friendship."

"Has the customer been back?" I asked.

"Quite often," he said.

"And have your tips improved?"

"You bet!"

Now this is not something I ask or expect from the waiters in our full-service restaurants. But what an impact one boy's hospitality made on that customer, who has become a cheerleader for our Dwarf House for life!

You can do a lot of things short of giving away

food to express hospitality, but the most important thing is to feel in your heart the desire to serve. If you really aren't interested in serving others, you don't need to be in the restaurant business in the first place. We like to say we recruit smiles. We can't teach a sour person to be joyful. Smiles are there because the heart is behind the smile.

Our restaurant team members are great ambassadors for the brand. They love to be out there with our customers, in the dining room, at the drive-thru, delivering food, or serving at events. Operators do a great job of choosing the employees who work with them.

—Dan Cathy, President and Chief Operating Officer, Chick-fil-A, Inc.

What we *can* do is suggest actions that put smiles on the faces of others. Nothing brings a smile quicker than service that goes beyond the expected. Several years ago I was in a Ritz Carlton hotel, and when I said, "Thank you," the man helping me smiled genuinely and replied, "My pleasure."

Those two words and that smile stayed in my thoughts for several days. "My pleasure." What a nice way of telling somebody you enjoyed serving them. Too often these days, especially in retail situations, when I say, "Thank you," the response is "No problem." Or worse, just a grunt. It seems the best I can hope for is, "You're welcome."

Following my experience at the Ritz Carlton, I asked our Operators, team members, and corporate

> **How Truett Did It**
> Truett always makes time for
> Operators, employees, customers,
> and vendors. He tells me, as an
> employee, what's on his heart,
> business or personal, and he says
> it with love and care.

headquarters employees to say, "My pleasure" whenever someone thanked them. The purpose was not just to change the words we say, but to remind those we serve, as well as ourselves, of the servant spirit and "second-mile" orientation we are continually building into our business. You expect that from a five-star hotel, but to have teenagers in a fast-food atmosphere saying it's their pleasure to

"My pleasure" is more than a requirement or an operating standard. It's more than a personal request from Truett. "My pleasure" is an expression from the heart of a team member, Operator, or staff member and literally shows that they want to go the extra mile. It's not perfunctory, not simply fulfilling an expectation, but it's an expression of hospitality. It shows that they care about the other person. They have enough value in the other person to go above and beyond—to exceed expectations. When that sort of servant spirit and second-mile service orientation is built into the team, they have that feeling with one another, not just the customer, and it can be powerfully motivating.

—Tim Tassopoulos
Senior Vice President,
Operations,
Chick-fil-A, Inc.

serve—that's a real head turner, and it pays great dividends. It distinguishes the individual and the company they represent.

I can't tell you how many letters we have received in the last five years from customers telling me how courteous our people are. "They even say 'my pleasure'!" many of them write.

Even though you are operating a big business, you need to run it like a small company and take advantage of the small things.

When I hear people say "my pleasure" on TV, it sounds nice, and it pays great dividends. We outperform other quick-service restaurant chains because of the courtesy and kindness we offer our customers. We advertise on radio, television, and in newspapers, but none of that takes the place of having customers as our cheerleaders.

Second-Mile Service

In recent years my son Dan, President and Chief Operating Officer of Chick-fil-A, Inc., has focused on taking the servant spirit of our people to a new level. We call it "Second-Mile Service." When customers come into a Chick-fil-A restaurant, they expect to be greeted with a smile. They expect delicious food delivered quickly and accurately in a clean environment. That's the *first* mile—the expectation.

Second-Mile Service is about the heart, and it goes above and beyond the requirements, making sure customers get not only what they expect, but something more that makes them say, "Wow!" It might be something the Operator plans: fresh flowers on tables, fresh ground pepper, or something as small as the toilet paper in the bathroom folded the way a nice hotel might.

Truett's goal is to be a good steward. To give. That's reflected in our Corporate Purpose. That's his focus.

—Perry Ragsdale
Senior Vice President,
Design and Construction,
Chick-fil-A, Inc.

Or it might be a team member or Operator responding to a particular situation, following his or her impulses in a surprising way. Almost every day we hear about a team member helping change a customer's tire or making an extra effort to return lost keys or a cell phone that was left behind. This is not a Chick-fil-A strategy, it's a way of life, and it shows us at our best.

A woman stopped at a Chick-fil-A restaurant in North Carolina and told the team member at the counter that she had left her pocketbook two hundred dred miles back, and she had another two hundred miles to go to her destination. She had no money for food or gas, so the team members gave her a meal and collected twenty-six dollars out of their own pockets and gave it to her for gas money.

Dad reminds us that people don't eat with us on Monday just because we were closed on Sunday. They eat with us because our food tastes good and we honor our customers.
—Bubba Cathy
Senior Vice President,
Chick-fil-A, Inc., and
President, Dwarf House, Inc.

These actions often run counter to our society, which has turned upside down since I started out in the restaurant business more than sixty years ago. Many teenagers are growing up in homes where they are not taught how to be courteous to others. Their world is filled with music that dishonors and disrespects.

Approximately 70 percent of the team members working in our restaurants across the country are younger than twenty-one years old. They have a heart for others, but in many cases they don't know

Why do you give away so many Be Our Guest cards?

—⁣ɯ⁣—

The Be Our Guest card, which you can redeem for a free Chick-fil-A menu item, is an extension of the sampling that we did from the first day we opened the first Chick-fil-A restaurants. We give away many thousands of them every year.

Be Our Guest cards create opportunities for us to have personal contact with potential customers and offer them an invitation to visit our restaurants. Nothing is more appealing than a personal invitation.

In new markets, the BOG card introduces people to our products and our restaurant. For those who already know us, a BOG creates goodwill in the same way as giving someone a plush Cow toy.

We could give a coupon for a dollar off instead, but who wants a dollar? They'll take the free food instead. It's a unique gift that they can get only from Chick-fil-A.

the right ways to express their hearts. With Second-Mile Service, we are introducing a concept to our teenagers that many of them have never experienced. We are developing extensive training programs, workshops, clinics, and motivational recognition, because we think Second-Mile Service will be powerful for our chain and for the people who work with us.

Dad has always been ahead of his time when it comes to building the brand. He gives a Be Our Guest card to anything that moves. And he always carries a shopping bag filled with Chick-fil-A plush Cows. While others might think that giving away so much is a shortsighted waste of money, Dad understands the return that will come from that investment.

—Dan Cathy, President and Chief Operating Officer, Chick-fil-A, Inc.

Courtesy pays dividends as much at the drive-thru window as it does over the counter inside. A national business magazine was doing an article on Chick-fil-A, and they wanted to get a photograph of me at a drive-thru window. We picked the quietest time of day, three-thirty in the afternoon, and went to a restaurant near our headquarters. We were there for an hour and a half, and business

If you're particularly proud of what you serve, you ought to tell people about it. You don't have to make a strong sales pitch. Just ask a simple question introducing the product: "Would you like to try our freshly squeezed lemonade?" When done politely and appropriately, customers appreciate the suggestion.

never slowed down enough at the drive-thru to get a picture of me without holding up traffic. It was very rewarding to see a steady flow of traffic at that time of day.

More than half of our sales occur at the drive-thru, so we concentrate on continually improving our service there. A lot of restaurant chains have sought to improve drive-thru service by using technological advances. We keep up with the latest technology, but our greatest improvements in service at the drive-thru, just like every other part of Chick-fil-A, are based on people. Operators establish goals for speed, and track order accuracy and customer loyalty, then they encourage their crews with incentives. Through the years we have tested packaging changes and technology, but as I say, the biggest impact on service is our people.

Truett is a roving promoter giving out Cows and Be Our Guest cards. He visits stores as a customer, then he comes back and gives us his feedback. He has the clearest vision on how the store should run, having operated a restaurant. Then he depends on us to keep it fresh.
—Bureon Ledbetter
Senior Vice President and General Counsel, Chick-fil-A, Inc.

How do you keep restaurants so clean?

—ᴡᴡ—

A lot of customers size up a restaurant by the cleanliness of its rest rooms. Keeping it clean doesn't require special skill, just discipline that comes from being concerned for the customer. You can take your cleaning supplies and be in and out of the bathroom in five minutes, but you won't have a clean bathroom. Doing it right means spending the time.

In the dining room, once again, keeping things clean requires no special skill— just an attentive eye for a table or chair that needs to be wiped and the discipline to do it now.

So I guess the bottom line is, our restaurants stay clean because we expect them to be clean. It's about as simple as that.

Operators choose their drive-thru leaders based on talent, character, and personality. The people wearing the headsets listening and talking to customers in their cars must have a sense of hospitality and a servant spirit, and at the same time they must have great attention to detail. They have to be efficient and enjoy working in an environment where there's a high emphasis on speed, accuracy, and service. A person who has all three of those attributes works well in the drive-thru team.

Truett is a living example of sowing and reaping. You have to offer samples all the time, give away Be Our Guest cards all the time. Truett is the most consistent role model of that principle in the business. He's challenged us by his example of keeping a bag of plush Cows in his car and BOGs in his pocket. You can give a free sample to almost anybody and you're a hero.

—Steve Robinson
Senior Vice President and
Chief Marketing Officer,
Chick-fil-A, Inc.

5
A Good Name

—⟋⟍—

In 2002 the United States Congress invited me to address a committee that was investigating "Oath Taking, Truth Telling, and Remedies in the Business World." Financial scandals at Enron, WorldCom, and other big public companies had hurt public confidence, and Congress was wondering what to do about business ethics.

Committee members said they were disturbed by illegal and questionable practices at those and other companies and by a "seemingly pervasive disregard of ethics by business executives and professionals."

The chairman conducting the meeting, Congressman Cliff Stearns said, "In the earnings race of the mid- to late Nineties, many business executives and professionals seem to have traded their own integrity and the good name of their company." Then he quoted Warren Buffett saying, "The attitudes and actions of the CEO and other officers of companies are what determine corporate conduct, good or bad."

You can be successful and honest at the same time.

I was reminded of the impact of a single Bible verse and an elementary school teacher. In the 1930s, my third-grade public school teacher required each of us to submit a verse, and each week she would put one verse on the blackboard. Then we would recite the Pledge of Allegiance and the Lord's Prayer in unison.

One Monday morning I submitted Proverbs 22:1, and that was the verse she selected. She wrote it on the blackboard with my name beside it, and all week long I saw that verse and my name. It made me feel special, and it led me to memorize the verse: "A good name is rather to be chosen than great riches, and loving favor rather than silver and gold."

Seventy years later I went to Capitol Hill to discuss what happens when people set aside character in search of great riches.

Chick-fil-A Corporate Purpose

To glorify God by being a faithful steward
of all that is entrusted to us.

To have a positive influence on all who
come in contact with Chick-fil-A.

"After agreeing to appear before you today," I said in my opening remarks, "I had to ask myself, 'What is the meaning of *business ethics*?' I concluded that there is really no such thing as business ethics. There is only personal ethics. I believe no amount of business school training or work experi-

> **How Truett Did It**
> Most companies boast a collegial atmosphere. Not Chick-fil-A! We have a loving atmosphere, where people serve each other because we truly love and care about each other. We are a family, and we love our product, our people, and our purpose.

ence can teach what is ultimately a matter of personal character. Businesses are not dishonest or selfish, people are. Thus, a business, successful or not, is merely a reflection of the character of its leadership.

We should ask ourselves what's
important and what's not important.
When you live by your convictions, people
respect that. It's important to be
consistent in living your convictions.

"I am deeply disturbed, as you are, by the lack of character I see in the marketplace. In order to satisfy the increased pressure for greater profits, some business leaders are making bad choices that ultimately hurt thousands of employees, stockholders, and the economy. We all know that the scorecard of

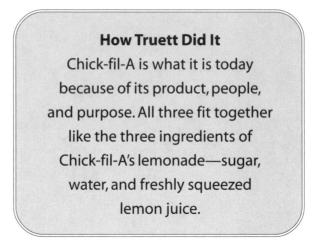

How Truett Did It
Chick-fil-A is what it is today because of its product, people, and purpose. All three fit together like the three ingredients of Chick-fil-A's lemonade—sugar, water, and freshly squeezed lemon juice.

any business is the profit it produces. Without profit, we cannot take care of our employees, our families, or contribute to the betterment of our communities. The question is, How do we balance the pursuit of profit and personal character? For me, I find that balance by applying Biblical principles. I see no conflict between Biblical principles and good business practices. We've tried to operate Chick-fil-A that way from the beginning."

You don't have to ask me, "How did you do it, Truett?" when it comes to maintaining a good reputation. Everybody knows the answer to that question. God gives each of us the answer in our hearts. We know what is right and what is wrong. When we choose the right thing, our reputation is enhanced. I was fortunate to have grown up in a time when public schools reinforced the understanding God gives us all.

Profit is not the name of the game. It is only the scorecard for some of our accomplishments.

One decision, perhaps, has affected our reputation more than any other. I don't remember much about the fourth Sunday in May 1946, except that I was tired. For weeks we had worked alongside carpenters, plumbers, and electricians to get the Dwarf Grill ready to open. Finally on Thursday, May 23, we opened the doors to customers, and we stayed open twenty-four hours a day. My brother Ben and I rotated twelve-hour shifts—and more. I lived in a rented room next door to the restaurant, and in those early days I only went home to sleep. Otherwise, I was in the restaurant. By midnight on Saturday I was exhausted. I can't remember ever being more thankful for a Sunday, a day to rest.

A lot of what we do is trust. The Chick-fil-A franchise Operator Agreement is based on trust. It's the biggest key to our success. Truett loves to be able to bring people around him he trusts so much, then he entrusts them with the image and reputation of the brand itself.
—Perry Ragsdale
Senior Vice President,
Design and Construction,
Chick-fil-A, Inc.

On that Sunday morning in 1946, it never occurred to me to open the restaurant. In fact, it would have been unusual for us to be open. Almost all businesses remained closed on Sundays in those days. We all recognized the need for a day of relaxation and to be with family, and many people spent at least part of the day worshiping the God who commanded His followers to set aside the Sabbath for rest. I took the time to go to church on Sunday morning and relax on Sunday afternoon and evening, and when I came back to work on Monday morning, I was refreshed and found it easier to greet our breakfast customers with a smile.

Twenty-one years later when we opened the first Chick-fil-A restaurant in Atlanta's Greenbriar Shopping Center in 1967, the mall was still closing every Sunday. After just a few years, though, mall developers and retailers across the country began to see Sunday as a day of shopping instead of a day of rest. Mall managers gave their tenants a choice of

> **How Truett Did It**
> Truett Cathy and Chick-fil-A are an honest voice that let their actions stand for themselves. Chick-fil-A gives hope that transparency is still an esteemed quality in business and in life.

whether to open on Sunday, and we chose to remain closed. It wasn't long, though, before those same managers wrote a clause in their contract with retailers that they must remain open seven days a week. We refused to sign such a contract, and our decision kept us from opening restaurants in some attractive malls around the country. Luckily, by that time our success had made Chick-fil-A attractive to mall developers even for just six days a week.

In recent years the question I've been asked more than any other is why we close on Sunday. When the malls asked us to open, it would have been easy to take advantage of that seventh day of the week and serve the millions of people across the country walking past our restaurants. Some have suggested that we lose a lot of money by closing on Sunday. After all, I've been told that 20 percent of all sales at other quick-serve chains are generated on Sunday.

I think that's the wrong way of looking at it. Everybody needs a break—Operators, their team members, our corporate headquarters staff. I also believe that the store itself needs a break. Even the equipment needs a rest after working hard for six days. The only way to make sure we all get at least one day off every week is to close. Companies that are open seven days a week may try to rotate days off so that everybody gets one day off every week. But if the business is open, you're going to be thinking about, it even if it's your day off. That takes away from your relaxation.

Closing on Sunday also gives us an advantage when we're hiring, because people like to know that they'll be guaranteed a day off every week to rest, spend time with their family and friends, and worship if they choose. Other companies may promise a day off every week, but if the company is

> **How Truett Did It**
> By living out the Corporate Purpose long before it was ever written down or thought of in those terms. Those two guiding principles are the foundation of the business.

open every day, the employee's day off might be on a Tuesday or a Thursday. Most people would rather be off on Sunday, when many of their friends and family members are also off.

Finally, we close on Sunday because we believe it is the right thing to do. America has changed dramatically since I started out in the restaurant business in 1946. But principles have not changed. I was teaching Sunday school to thirteen-year-old boys one week, and I asked, "What would you think if you knew that my cash registers were jingling while I was teaching this lesson on the observance of the Lord's Day?"

One boy answered, "I would think you are a hypocrite."

That sizes it up pretty well.

I believe the record has proved us correct. Closing on Sunday turned out to be the best business decision I ever made. We generate more sales in our restaurants in six days than many other chains do in seven. So I tell our customers, "You eat with us six days a week, and I'll give you permission to eat somewhere else on Sundays."

6
PEOPLE FIRST

—⚬—

From the earliest days at the Dwarf House we had good people who worked with us, some of them for so long our children thought of them as aunts and uncles. Zelma Calhoun worked in our kitchen for more than forty-five years. I can't take a bite of a Chick-fil-A Lemon Pie without thinking of Zelma. For all those years in the original Dwarf House, she made all of our Lemon Pies by hand, about seventy a day. Through the years she made more than 650,000 pies!

Then we had Annie McGruder, Zelma's younger sister, who worked in the Dwarf House almost as long. Betty Dial was a waitress for forty years. Henry White worked for us for forty years, and Paul Richards managed the Dwarf House for more than thirty years.

An Atlanta newspaper reporter interviewed Zelma when she was about to retire, and he asked what made her so loyal. "I've never heard Mr. Cathy raise his voice," she said. "I don't remember him arguing with anybody. I've never heard him tell somebody to do something. He would ask. He'd say, 'Zelma, would you make me such-and-such a pie? Is that a problem?' Well, you had to do it, because he asked so nice."

> **How Truett Did It**
> By creating a culture that sets, expects, and rewards high standards and performance.

We felt like a family, and in many cases we have actually had family members working together. In addition to Zelma and her sister Annie both working in the Dwarf House for decades, their other sister, Josephine Murphy, and their mother also worked with us. Some companies have rules against hiring relatives of employees, but many of our Operators hire the siblings of good team members

to work in their restaurants. I think that can be a
good idea. A hardworking teenager probably grew
up in a family where hard work and respect are
expected. You can expect brothers and sisters to be
the same way. And one of my greatest pleasures is
when the child of an Operator wants to own and
operate a Chick-fil-A
restaurant.

When we have
team members working
together like a family,
they extend that
feeling to their custom-
ers. When Paul
Richards was manager
of the Dwarf House, he
mailed out about four
hundred birthday cards
with handwritten
notes to customers
every year. He visited
them when they were
sick and sent food when there was an illness or
death. Customers knew we cared.

That's really the key: caring. In 1992 the Caring

*Dad's love of people is a great
motivator. We need to nurture
and care for that perspective.
Sometimes we allow our egos to
get over-inflated, and we need to
relate back to Dad's mindset—
to glorify God, not praise ourselves, and to put other people
before ourselves.*
—Bubba Cathy
Senior Vice President,
Chick-fil-A, Inc., and
President, Dwarf House, Inc.

Institute presented me with its National Caring Award. The mission of the Caring Institute includes the statement: "the solution to most problems is the caring of one human being for another." That's been my experience.

Building Long-Term Relationships

Of course, to be successful in business, you have to do more than care about other people. The most important decision we make at Chick-fil-A is selecting restaurant Operators who care about others, who can motivate their team, and who understand how to run a business. Our franchise Operators determine the success of the chain. They're the ones meeting customers and selling chicken sandwiches.

We expect our relationship with our Operators to last a very long time. Many of our Operators stay with us for twenty years or more, and fewer than 5 percent, on average, leave the system in any given year through retirement or other reasons.

We currently open fewer than one hundred restaurants each year, and we have thousands of people applying to be Operators. That allows us to be extremely selective. We choose about two-thirds of our Operators from among the team members

Truett is an extremely good delegator. He didn't give me many instructions. He did tell me, "I want you to help me open restaurants and see that they stay open." The emphasis was on stay open. That sank in. Anybody can open a restaurant. All it takes is money. But keeping one open is what makes the difference. If you open each restaurant knowing you can't just close them if they don't work out, you're more careful about how you build them, where you build them, and who you put in there to run them. It's extremely good business strategy to think in those terms.

> *—Jimmy Collins*
> *Former President,*
> *Chick-fil-A, Inc.*

who have been working in Chick-fil-A restaurants. These are people who understand our principles and our operations. We like to say they've grown up with us.

Ideally, we select Operators from the communities in which the restaurant is going to be located, where they already have connections: family, friends, business relationships, and social relationships. Operators are tied into the community, and we encourage them to capitalize on that. We not only gain business opportunities from that, we also get opportunities to make a contribution to the community. It's a two-way street. People like to do business with folks who are making a contribution, whether it is to their school, their church, or their club. It creates a lot of goodwill for Chick-fil-A.

We look for several important traits in Operators: strong entrepreneurial spirit; desire to be in

Truett communicates his passion not with memos and policy manuals, but with the stories he tells. He is a terrific storyteller, and he knows how to use those stories to communicate a message of quality.
—Jimmy Collins
Former President,
Chick-fil-A, Inc.

business for yourself but not by yourself; willingness to operate the restaurant on a full-time basis; the ability to lead and influence others in a positive way; and results-oriented self-starters.

The Operator selection process can be lengthy, sometimes as long as a year, because we want to be certain before we make a franchise commitment that we believe the relationship will last. That means knowing the applicant and making sure that the applicant understands Chick-fil-A and our culture.

Selecting the Right People

The selection of people who work in the individual Chick-fil-A restaurants is made by the Operators, and the best ones get involved in their communities, churches, and schools, where they meet and get to know potential team members. Good Operators always keep their eyes open for new people. You never know where you might meet the right person—one who will be a good employee and might someday become a fellow Operator.

One day I stopped to buy peaches from a man selling from his pickup truck on Tara Boulevard near my home. Tom was well-mannered and polite, and I learned in talking with him that he went to the orchard and picked out the peaches he wanted to sell.

I looked through a basket and noticed that the peaches at the bottom were just as nice as the ones on top. Usually, when I bought peaches at the farmer's market, they put the prettiest, ripest peaches on top and the knobby green ones on bottom.

Operators don't feel like their relationship is with a company. They feel like their relationship is with Truett. He's done a good job of trying to extend that feeling throughout the chain with long-term relationships.
—Bureon Ledbetter
Senior Vice President and
General Counsel,
Chick-fil-A, Inc.

Tom was applying the same principle to selling peaches on the side of the road that we exercise in our Chick-fil-A restaurants: be kind to the customers and give them a product they're pleased with so they'll come back. I knew he had a lot to offer, and I told him, "Someday I want you to come to work for Chick-fil-A."

Tom Pike has now been a franchise Operator for more than twenty-five years.

Truett surrounds himself with people who know what they're doing and have his values. He doesn't fret over what they do. They know what they're supposed to do. He trusts you, but he makes sure you trust yourself. He'll challenge you on anything. He wants to be sure of your conviction— that you've considered the upsides and downsides.

—Steve Robinson
Senior Vice President and
Chief Marketing Officer,
Chick-fil-A, Inc.

Almost every day I am reminded that you can see the signs of quality early. When I meet a sixteen-year-old, I can tell pretty quickly if he or she has the potential to be an Operator someday. I'm guilty of making up my mind in the first two minutes about that. A firm handshake and a great smile

> **How Truett Did It**
> With faith in God and mankind, Truett treats others as he would like to be treated and gives God the glory. Abundant blessings for all pour forth.

go a long way, and I expect a teenager to look me in the eye. How you present yourself is very important. You should dress neatly, keep yourself clean, and have a nice haircut.

Years ago I was looking for a chief financial officer at Chick-fil-A, and I learned of a man who lived nearby and had graduated number two in his class from law school. He had also passed the CPA exam, and he looked just like what we needed. I

We gradually become a part of those people we associate with, whether good or bad. If you want to be a great preacher, you associate with other great preachers, and something rubs off on you. If you want to be a great businessman, you associate with other great businessmen, and something rubs off on you. For instance, my sons have been associated with me all of their lives, and look at them. Both of them are going bald.

called him and set up a meeting, and when I got to the place, he didn't bother to get up out of his chair. Then he gave me a limp handshake. I knew right away that I wouldn't want that guy on my staff. I went through with the interview, but my mind was made up.

Truett leads by example—by the way he lives. He is so transparent in living out his beliefs, we see it daily. He has led us that way.

—Perry Ragsdale
Senior Vice President,
Design and Construction,
Chick-fil-A, Inc.

Another time I asked someone if he would be interested in becoming a Chick-fil-A Operator. "I'll give it a try," he said.

Well, that's not good enough. You can't just give it a try. We expect our franchise relationships with our Operators to last a very long time. If you don't plan to be here in ten years or longer, we would rather not have you in the first place. We present a business opportunity to Operators, but it's up to the Operators to hire and manage employees, generate sales, and control costs. You can't do that well if you're just giving it a try. Many of our Operators stay with us for twenty years or more, and some have been with Chick-fil-A for more than thirty-five years.

*Businesses don't
succeed or fail.*

People do.

Our relationship with our Operators begins with the assumption that we have the same goals and we all plan to succeed. Our Operators own their own businesses, but our relationship is extremely close. Our financial arrangement reflects our closely aligned interests and is different from a lot of other franchise relationships.

Truett doesn't see Chick-fil-A as a platform for his faith. He applies faith principles to the business.
—Tim Tassopoulos
Senior Vice President,
Operations,
Chick-fil-A, Inc.

We do not require a large up-front franchise fee. We don't need an Operator's money; we need his or her abilities, experience, passion, and desire to serve others. A Chick-fil-A Operator makes only a $5,000 working capital deposit for the opportunity to own a franchise. Then the Operator pays monthly 15 percent of gross sales for trademark licensing and other services such as marketing and operations support. After paying the costs of running the restaurant—salaries, food, utilities, etc.— the Operator then pays Chick-fil-A 50 percent of his or her restaurant's profits.

We've used this same arrangement since we

opened our first restaurant in 1967, and it still works. Operators are motivated to generate sales, and we're motivated to support them in that effort. The result has been extremely profitable for them and for us. Under our arrangement, an Operator can earn an outstanding profit from a single restaurant.

Many people have asked me why we would create an opportunity for a restaurant Operator to earn so much money without having to invest the capital to build the restaurant. The answer is easy. The more money the Operator earns, the more Chick-fil-A earns. The shared goals and opportunity works for all of us.

You talk to Truett and you never doubt that you have his full attention. Some people never learn how. Some people let you talk. Some people listen. We all know the difference. Truett Cathy will listen.

—Jimmy Collins
Former President,
Chick-fil-A , Inc.

Supporting the People Who Sell Chicken

Jimmy Collins, our President for many years, often told people working at Chick-fil-A, "If you're not selling chicken, you'd better be supporting

The first thing you see about Truett is his heart. What people don't see about him sometimes is the sharp businessman that he is. He comes across as very disarming, trusting, warm, and down to earth. From a business standpoint, however, Truett is sharp and perceptive. He doesn't want to pore over numbers and charts. He wants us to tell him how we're doing, and he listens intently. He hears between the lines. We're talking about different aspects of business, and his questions show remarkable insight about where we are and where we're going. He sees through to the reasons about why things are happening and brings a unique business insight.

—Perry Ragsdale
Senior Vice President,
Design and Construction,
Chick-fil-A, Inc.

somebody who is." It was an effective reminder we don't have any cash registers at the Chick-fil-A headquarters.

In building our support staff, we have made some of our most important decisions in business. I wanted to surround myself with people who knew

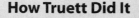

How Truett Did It
The leadership at Chick-fil-A hires high caliber people who possess both strong ethics and stellar talent. They then empower those people to do their jobs with commitment to them as individuals.

what they were doing and also shared my values. It was a slow process. Sometimes it took many months to be sure we had the right person. We take that long because when we hire somebody for the corporate office, we want a long-term relationship. The commitment to making the right decisions

Many entrepreneurs I've been involved with exert too much direct control on the organization. A lot of times you get the impression people are afraid to tell the owner the real truth; they're afraid of the owner's reaction. It's difficult to disagree with a tyrant; the consequences can be severe. With Truett Cathy, there is none of that. We don't disagree often, but I feel completely relaxed when I take an exactly opposite viewpoint from him. It's always a respectful disagreement. You relate to him the same way he relates to you— with love, appreciation, and respect. He respects you, and you feel it. You sense it. That is very different from many people in power. You may experience their toler- ance but not their respect. With Truett Cathy you feel his respect even if he absolutely disagrees.

> *—Buck McCabe*
> *Senior Vice President and*
> *Chief Financial Officer,*
> *Chick-fil-A, Inc.*

paid off. After more than twenty years our Executive Committee, which is our company's top leadership, remains unchanged except for the retirement of President Jimmy Collins.

When we get away for a two- or three-day business retreat, we begin by sharing personal concerns and praying together, and we pray for God's guidance. It's an important bonding time that says we are in one accord in what we do. We don't have conflict in our Executive Committee meetings.

Truett is decidedly nonconfrontational. Confrontation is usually caused by disappointment, and we work hard to avoid disappointing people.

—Bureon Ledbetter
Senior Vice President
and General Counsel,
Chick-fil-A, Inc.

That doesn't mean we don't disagree. If you have two people who agree on everything, one person is unnecessary. We prosper by debating ideas and voicing our opinions. But ultimately we have to make a decision.

Sometimes, but not often, I am thoroughly convinced that the decision I have made is the right one, even though it differs from the others, and I will exercise my authority to approve or reject a decision against their wishes. In most cases, though, if we can't agree on something, a better idea is to table the decision rather than to exercise the power.

7

THE RIGHT LOCATION

—⚂—

Selecting a good location for a restaurant doesn't guarantee success, but a bad location can put you out of business. The lot where I chose to build the Dwarf House turned out to be a great choice. Ford Motor Company was building a new assembly plant across the street from that location, giving me the opportunity to build a base of regular customers.

In our first year in business we fed many of the construction workers, and for forty-nine years, until the Ford plant closed in 2006, we fed thousands of Ford employees. Also, Delta Air Lines has its headquarters in Hapeville next to the Atlanta airport, and over the years many Delta workers and executives have become Dwarf House regulars. Other airline and airport employees also ate with us almost every day.

Twenty-one years later my sister Gladys had a gift shop in Atlanta's first enclosed shopping mall, Greenbriar Shopping Center, a few miles away from the Dwarf House. She noticed that the only places to eat in the mall were sit-down restaurants—there was no place for a quick meal—and she suggested that I lease space in the mall to sell our new chicken sandwich.

Truett, Jimmy, and Bureon never got too excited about any one deal to compromise what we would pay. They were willing to say no, even to a great mall. So we had some of the most consistent good deals in the business, and that kept down the cost of operation.
—Steve Robinson
Senior Vice President and Chief Marketing Officer, Chick-fil-A, Inc.

The advantages of a mall location appeared obvious. We wouldn't have to sink a lot of capital into real estate, and we would have thousands of potential customers walking right past our front counter.

I had my eye on a space left vacant when a hearing aid store closed. It was tiny, only thirteen feet wide and less than thirty feet deep. The mall said it was 384 square feet, but I knew it would be big enough for people to come to the counter and place an order.

First I had to convince the mall developer to let me in. He was afraid of the mess our customers would leave behind and the smell we would generate when we cooked. We showed the Greenbriar developer how we would vent all of the fumes straight out through the ceiling, and we also convinced him that there was almost no food waste from our meals.

He gave us an opportunity, and we opened in November 1967. Within a few months we were already generating more than ten times our base rent because of our strong sales.

We faced the same problem for several years. Enclosed shopping malls were going up all over, but almost every developer we approached was skeptical of a fast-food operation.

Our sales record at Greenbriar helped open opportunities at other malls, and eventually our pioneering would lead other fast-food chains to open in malls.

In the early years shopping malls didn't have

food courts, so our restaurants were right alongside other stores. And every mall was different, so no two Chick-fil-A spaces were alike. Our early mall restaurants were 1,200 to 1,500 square feet, much larger than our first restaurant, so we had room inside for tables and seats for fifty or sixty customers.

Truett has a keen understanding of the need to create consistency for customers.
—Jimmy Collins
Former President,
Chick-fil-A

We wanted to keep customer lines as short as possible, so we put as many cash registers as we could across the counter. As soon as customers stepped into our restaurant, instead of finding the end of a long line, we wanted them to make eye contact with a smiling face and a team member asking, "May I help you?"

Our goal when we designed the restaurants was to keep the homey atmosphere and also look substantial. Even though we were brand new, we looked like we had been there for a while and were going to stay here for a long time. Jimmy Collins, who would eventually become President of Chick-fil-A, and Perry Ragsdale, who came to work with us as a draftsman, continued to use standard red shingles over the menu board and in front of the store. We also continued to put salads and pies in a case on the counter for customers to see, and we did the cooking out front in plain view of customers in all of our early restaurants.

Through the years as we made changes to space behind the counter, we drew those changes up on paper then went into our warehouse and built a "restaurant" out of foam core, an Exacto knife, and hot glue. Then we went through all the motions of cooking and serving customers and determined which design would work best.

We also had our design people spend a lot of time in the field talking with Operators and seeing how they ran their businesses. Experienced Operators know better than anybody how to serve people quickly and efficiently.

It's interesting that the success of Chick-fil-A actually helped lead to the creation of mall food courts. Chick-fil-A was the first restaurant brand that showed up repeatedly in malls, and our success must have had developers scratching their heads and wondering if they might be missing an opportunity to sell more food.

With more and more restaurants wanting to get

into malls, mall developers decided to put all the food in one central area. We didn't like the food court idea at first, because it meant giving up our in-store seating. Our customers would have to sit out in the mall area, where we depended on the mall staff to maintain a quality environment. Mall managers were not food people primarily, and we would rather have kept customers in our own restaurant where we were responsible for seating, cleaning—the whole atmosphere.

We held on to our own seating for a while, but eventually we conformed and became part of the food courts with no seats of our own. Mall developers improved their efficiency in running food courts, and the system now works well for us.

Moving to the food court and into a much smaller space also created new marketing challenges. Now Chick-fil-A stands alongside McDonald's, Wendy's, and other well-known national chains. Competing for our share of customers in that environment with a sixteen- to eighteen-foot-wide storefront makes store and menu board design even more critical. We have very little room for posters and additional messages to customers, so we have learned to use messages on bags, boxes, and cups more effectively.

More than ever, we rely on our reputation and the previous positive experiences of our customers so that when they walk into the food court, they look for Chick-fil-A.

BEYOND THE MALL

By the mid-1980s we had 330 restaurants in malls. Developers were building fewer malls than they had through the 1970s, and the slowdown in mall development was projected to continue. Our goal at that time was to double our sales over the next five years, so we had to create opportunities beyond the mall environment.

At the same time we had a lot of people telling us, "I would eat more frequently with you if it were more convenient." In 1984 we asked Tim Tassopoulos, currently Senior Vice President, Operations for Chick-fil-A, to investigate the possibility of building Chick-fil-A restaurants out on the street. These stand-alone restaurants would cost roughly twice as much to build and open as a mall restaurants, but we believed stand-alone locations also had the potential to generate at least twice as much revenue.

We moved deliberately, opening our first stand-alone location in Atlanta in 1986. The new location offered new challenges and opportunities. We expected sales at stand-alone locations to be more consistent throughout the year. In the malls traffic can vary significantly depending on the shopping season.

Moving out of the malls also changed the way we saw—literally—our competition. The first store

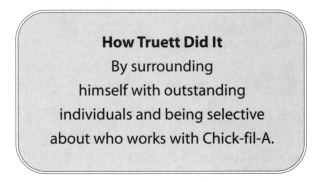

How Truett Did It
By surrounding himself with outstanding individuals and being selective about who works with Chick-fil-A.

was in sight of McDonald's, Arby's and Burger King. These were the days before the food court, so it was the first time we had gone head-to-head with our competitors on our doorstep like that.

Opening outside the mall also allowed us to serve full breakfast for the first time and longer dinner hours.

Our primary development focus remained on

the malls; we opened twenty-six mall restaurants and only one stand-alone restaurant in 1986. In 1988 we built five stand-alone restaurants, all in metro Atlanta, where we could watch them closely and learn from them. After twenty years exclusively in the malls, we had a lot to learn about our new environment. Then we slowly expanded our presence with these street-location restaurants, striving to make good decisions each time. A decade later, in 1998, our focus had shifted almost exclusively to stand-alone restaurants, with forty-seven opened and only five new restaurants opened in malls.

It's hard to say which challenges came first, but real estate and construction issues, beginning with site selection, have to rank among them. When we came out of the mall environment, we had never dealt with building exteriors—just interior finish work. Perry Ragsdale, our Senior Vice President, Design and Construction, had a dream of developing a single set of architectural plans that we could use for all of our restaurants. We quickly found out that's not the way it works. Every county and municipal development department and every piece of property has its own issues.

We brought in a design firm to help us create an architectural look that suited our image. They designed the building as well as signs, lighting and other aspects of the Chick-fil-A "look."

With these freestanding units we had to maintain parking lots, heating and air-conditioning, and other systems that had been maintained by mall owners. As the number of stand-alone restaurants grew, we created a facilities management team to work with Operators to keep the restaurants fresh.

BE OUR GUEST

From a day-to-day operational standpoint, running a stand-alone restaurant isn't so different from a mall unit. The biggest challenge we faced was bringing customers into the restaurant. That was the challenge for our Senior Vice President of Marketing and Chief Marketing Officer, Steve Robinson, and his group. You see, in a mall, we have thousands of people walking past our restaurant every day—a captive audience. From our first day with our first restaurant, we invited customers in with free samples of our product, "Be Our Guest" cards, and point-of-sale displays with slogans like "Taste It. You'll Love It for Good®," all of which generate an almost immediate response.

Because most of the people passing our stand-alone restaurants are in cars, it doesn't make as much sense to hand out samples. So we encouraged our Operators to become even more involved in their communities, visiting nearby businesses and giving away even more Be Our Guest cards. Operators also support community schools, churches, and civic organizations. The result has been a growing positive impact across the country.

FINAL NOTE
HOW DID *We* DO IT?

The title of this book is *How Did You Do It, Truett?* I hope that after reading it you understand I didn't do it. *We* did. From opening day at the Dwarf Grill in 1946, I have never been alone. My brother and business partner Ben worked alongside me until his untimely death in 1948 in a plane crash. By that time we had a talented and dedicated crew.

After we were married, my wife, Jeannette, spent countless hours helping run the restaurant. And our children have also been an important part of the business. Dan likes to tell people he has been in the restaurant business since nine months before he was born.

Today we have more than 50,000 people across the United States dedicated to the success of Chick-fil-A. I am grateful to every one of them. Working side-by-side, *we* did it.

Eleven Do's and Don'ts of Proven Success

1. *Don't be burdened with personal debt.*
    a. *Car payment*
    b. *House payment*
    c. *Establish a nest egg*
    d. *Live simple*

2. *Start early as a teenager. Concentrate on what brings you happiness in your career. Have a tremendous "want to"— determination.*

3. *Sacrifice material things. Reward yourself later.*

4. *Shortcut to success: Observe what is working in the lives of others. Teenagers, observe mature individuals.*

5. *Don't try to please all people.*

6. Set priorities in the proper order.

7. Expand cautiously. Grow your business cautiously.

8. Franchising may or may not be good for your particular business. Use it cautiously.

9. Be prepared for disappointments. Many successful individuals experience failure.

10. Be kind to people. Courtesy is very cheap but brings great dividends.

11. Invite God to be involved in every decision. God gives us a brain to use— common sense. You can do it if you want to. God has given each of us a talent. Maybe yours is yet to be discovered. We honor God with our success. He designed us to be winners.